There's A Jewel

In You

VOLUME 3

FROM TRIALS TO TRIUMPH

RELENTLESS
PUBLISHING

Enjoy Chapter 2

There's A Jewel In You, Volume 3 : From Trials To Triumph
Copyright © 2019 by Chantea M. Williams

Published by :
Relentless Publishing House, LLC
www.relentlesspublishing.com

ISBN: 978-1-948829-30-4

First Edition: May 2019

10 9 8 7 6 5 4 3 2 1

CONTENTS

INTRODUCTION

FROM TRIALS TO TRIUMPH, is the story of many teen mothers who decided not to give up on life. The journey of motherhood at a young age is full of many trials. Unfortuantely, some don't have the support necessary to pull themselves together and overcome the stastics of a teenage mother.

The National Conference of State Legislatures reports on their site (**http://www.ncsl.org/research/health/teen-pregnancy-prevention.aspx**):

- *Only about half of teen mothers earn a high school diploma by age 22, compared to 90 percent of women without a teen birth. Teenage mothers are also more likely to live in poverty and depend on public assistance. Children born to teen parents are more likely to have lower school achievement, enter the child welfare and correctional systems, drop out of high school and become teen parents themselves, compared to children born to older parents.*

- *Thirty percent of teenage girls who drop out of high school cite pregnancy or parenthood as a primary reason. This rate is even higher for Hispanic and African-American teens, at nearly 40 percent.*
- *Only about half of women ages 20-29 who gave birth as a teen have a high school diploma, compared to 90 percent of women ages 20-29 who did not have a teen birth.*
- *And among those who have a baby before age 18, about 40 percent finish high school and fewer than 2 percent finish college by age 30.*
- *Older teens account for about 70 percent of all teen births. Pregnancy among this age group can disrupt young people's educational and career goals, as older teens are often finishing high school and entering the job market, or pursuing postsecondary education. Sixty-one percent of students who have a child after enrolling in community college fail to complete their degree. This dropout rate is 65 percent higher than for those who do not have children during community college.*

They dream just like any other teenager of doing great things with their life and being successful when they grow up. For some, their dreams are put on hold umtil they are stable enough to pursue them and for others, their dreams will never become a reality.

Unfortunately, they believe the lies that their life is now over and they will never have the opportunity to do anything but to try and be a good mother to their child. No one chooses to speak life into them and encourage them to keep pressing forward because they never see past the title of a teenage mother.

I experienced this first hand as a sophomore in high school and a 15-year-old teenage mother. I had a teacher who refused to pass me for the nine weeks, even though I did all my work that was sent home to me, just because I was not present in the class. He told me that he didn't think it was fair to give me a passing grade. What he really was saying is that I was going to be anything any way so why should it matter. What he really was saying was I don't see anyting but a failure in you so what does it really matter. What he really was saying is that you will never be successful in life or even probably graduate high school so what does it really matter. Well, what he didn't understand was that it mattered to me. I was not going to allow his opinion or misperception of me because of my sitatuion dictate my life or my future. What did I do? I passed his class for the year and graduated on time.

In our anthology series, There's A Jewel In You, we are dispelling the statistics and proving that despite the choice we made that led us to become young mothers, we still chose to be get back up when everyone else wanted us to stay down after the count. It is our desire that every young mother who reads our stories, will believe they too can be successful in life and take the necessary steps in order to make it happen for them. We also hope that as teen girls read our stories, they will make choices with their lives and not follow down the same path we journeyed on.

We want you to learn the lessons from our lives and choose to be greater. You hold the power to your lives and the thoughts you have about yourself will determine where you go in life and the things you accomplish. You are worth the wait! Repeat this statement outloud: **I AM WORTH THE WAIT! MY PURPOSE DESERVES A CHANCE WITHOUT ANY DELAY. I AM ALREADY DESTINED FOR GREATNESS!**

To all the young mothers who will read our stories, always remember YOU ARE STILL SOMEBODY! Your dreams are still possible and you owe it to yourself and your child(ren) to be the best you can be at all times. There is a JEWEL in you so let it shine brightly!

~Chantea M. Williams

1

THE FRAGRANT SMELL OF FRIED ONIONS
and cilantro filled the hallways of the major corporation
where I serve as Executive Chef. With the weight of the
entire kitchen on my shoulders, I excel in my role as
Executive Chef and carry the honor of being the first
female ever to walk in these shoes. I fought for this role
and took what was rightfully mine; this achieved by me!
This woman in a male dominated field. Once I was called
"Camille", now as Commander in Chief, I'm called "Chef";
who'd have thought?

As I sit at my desk in my very own corporate office,
I reflect over my journey to get to where I am today; that
moment where it all began and the challenges, I overcame

that have shaped me.

I was the middle child of my parent's three girls, the hardheaded, sassy one. As a high school freshman, I'd had a year full of fighting and skipping school. My only goal and focus then was to be popular. By sophomore year I'd achieved my goal of being popular, and had now earned a name for myself. My virginity was out the window and I was absolutely fearless!

I can recall hanging out with my friend Ashley one sunny day in September. Ashley was a member of a local gang called the bloods and though she was only 5 feet tall, she could fight her behind off. We'd become friends during my freshman year and it was common practice for us to hit the corner store for a social hour. It was the hangout spot most times. I was really cute that day. My auntie was a hairdresser so my hair was freshly relaxed and laid, cut into a cute bob with a bang I was wearing a black mini skirt and a hot pink tank top. Ashley and I got our snacks and while leaving the store, bumped into a friend of Ashleys who she introduced as Pooh blood. Pooh was about 6'2", skinny, and dark chocolate complexion. I wasn't' immediately attracted to Pooh, but that meeting changed my life. Ashley told me that he wanted to talk to me and gave me his beeper number. My only interest was whether or not he had money; Ashley confirmed that he did, and that was all that I needed.

Early on I realized the power that I had in between my legs. I knew that my friends would get sneakers, jewelry, clothes and shopping sprees in return for sex from boyfriends or guys that liked them, so I was going to test that theory out. My parents didn't even allow me to talk on the phone to boys. If a male called mom would say "Camille can't talk to boys on the phone." How embarrassing. I cared less. So that night I beeped pooh. I turned the ringer off of my parent's phone so that when the phone rang in their room they didn't hear it. This would help me to speak on the phone without interruption. I had a strategy and it worked. I talked to pooh that night nothing super special but then the next day he was outside of my school hanging out.

My high school was the spot to hang out after school and a lot of gangbangers came to be seen and to protect their set that was still in high school. Pooh made it a habit of coming to see me after school, which turned into me skipping classes, which later turned into me skipping school. I wasn't a newbie to skipping school. I can recall my first time. My best friend lived with her grandmother who worked during the day. One day on our way to school she suggested that we skip. Go watch TV and eat some snacks at her place. That sounded good to me. So, we skipped and no one ever knew. In time Pooh and I got closer. Everyone knew who he was because he was a well-known gang banger around the city. I started wearing red and black all the time.

After school strolls to the park turned into stops at Jimmy's Army and Navy to buy me things. My first purchase was a pair of red Timberland boots with a black sole. That helped me to continue to match the red and black beads he placed around my neck. I had the protection of the bloods. I became increasingly active in sex. There wasn't even any real wining or dining. I mean we were kids. The sweetest thing he did was come to my school had me called down to the office and handed me balloons that said I love you, a pooh bear teddy bear and a gold bracelet inscribed, I love you. The night before on the phone I told him that I loved him. He didn't say it back but the next afternoon he put his money to work. He didn't have a job but he worked the streets with his gang. Selling drugs, a lifestyle that maybe he was forced into based off his own upbringing.

That night we sealed the deal and that was probably the night I got pregnant. He was mine and I was his. Puppy love. November came around and I remember taking a group picture with some friends of mine. Say cheese! I couldn't wait for the picture to be over fast enough to go to the bathroom. Was I pregnant I thought to myself? A couple of weeks later my questions were confirmed. My cycle never came. I went to the teen health center at school to get a test and surely, I was pregnant. He was so happy. Why? What are you nuts? I was numb. I think that I was so focused on being grown that it didn't faze me that I could get pregnant.

Everything started to taste different. Those Newport's I used to smoke I couldn't smoke anymore. Yuck. They didn't even taste the same. I couldn't tell my mom or my sisters so I kept it hidden. My friends and everyone at school knew I was pregnant. Days turned into weeks then into months and I reach 19 weeks but I was small and still able to hide it. I wore sweatshirts and long-sleeved baggy shirts all the time. My friend's mom offered to bring me to get an abortion. I never thought about that. I was going to have my baby! By this time Pooh and I had fallen apart, not for any particular reason, we just did. Just the way things are sometimes. He checked on me and promised to be there for the baby. We didn't talk as much as we did before because he was in and out of jail.

Sometimes a few days sometimes a few weeks. I got tired of trying to find him.

One day in school the nurse called me down to the office. She told me that I had to tell my mother I was 19 weeks and still had not received prenatal care. I could not tell my mom. I knew that she would be furious. This was not my first pregnancy. At 14, I got pregnant and miscarried. My mom expects more from me. So surely, she would be upset with me. Nonetheless, I agreed with the nurse and we picked a time to call my mom. The nurse and I picked a time to call my mom. She said she would help me to tell her and be my support.

Therefore, the next day the meeting happened. We called my mom over the phone and told her. She was furious of course. She came right up to the school. I was in biology class. The class I shined in. When my mom arrived, my biology teacher began to rave about how great of a student I was. My mom had asked me to come out to her. I was so petrified to go out and speak to her that I refused to come out of class. Girl, you better get your butt out here before I drag you out. That's all I needed to hear. I was embarrassed enough. I packed up my things swung my book bag over my shoulder and met my mother in the hallway. She began to fuss at me as we walk to the nurse's office.

We called Planned Parenthood and learned that 19 weeks was the cut off for abortion. I couldn't be seen! The meeting ended and we went home where mom continued to scream and holler. She was beyond hurt and angry. She was pissed off. She told me that she was finding a home for me to live in down south to have the baby. I couldn't stay with her. My dad came home from work and found out about the pregnancy. He didn't say much. He was totally upset. Time went on and I found out that Pooh had been unfaithful. At my first prenatal visit, they told me that I had contracted a STD. How embarrassing! I also found out that I was carrying a boy. Needless to say, that was the end of us. The relationship was over. As the months went on, I talked to my son's father less and less. Barely even knowing where he was.

My mom begins to accept that I was pregnant and as a family, we move forward. I saw him one more time before I had the baby. I was about six months pregnant. I handed him a brochure and circled a few things that I wanted for the baby. He never got to buy them because he was arrested and this time put away for a long time. I had to figure out how life would go after I gave birth. Would I stay in school? Would I drop out? The high school that I attended had a child care program. Students could apply to be a part of this program and if accepted your child could actually come to school with you. Daycare was on the first floor of the building and every mom was able to have one. This gave them the opportunity to be with a child and actually learn how to take care of the baby's safety, feeding, and teach us all baby things. I applied and took the last spot for the fall of 2001.

My mom really began to nurture me and help me to prepare for birth. She taught me how to dress and took me shopping for maternity clothes. She also encouraged me to pack lunches and snacks for school because I would be hungry during the day. In summer 2001 right before school started, I had my son Quinton Amir. He came into the world on August 21 and was 7 lbs. 11 oz. and 21 inches long. I couldn't go back to school right away, so the Board of Education sent a teacher to my house while I healed for six weeks. Having my son was tough. I had an amazing amount of support from my parents physically and financially. They helped me to take care of him, while I focused on school.

When school started for us, a little yellow bus would come and get us. We left school daily a half an hour earlier than everyone else for safety reasons. My room turned into a nursery and slowly I became comfortable with being a mom. My grades were great. I got my first job as a cashier at a grocery store and finally was able to help financially take care of my son. My parents didn't really put pressure on me. They continue to help out and take care of us. I realized that I would be doing this without my son's father who was still in prison.

High school continued to go the same for the rest of that year. I entered into my senior year focused one day on my way to work I met this guy he was older than me but he showed interest in me. He asked me out on a date right on the spot. Something I've never experienced or even heard of. He was driving a candy apple red Range Rover and wearing Versace shades. "Cha-Ching," I thought. I was all about the money. I accepted.

That night he picks me up from work and we went to the diner for a date. That was all she wrote I started to date this guy and he was a lot older but out of his mouth, he said he was only 10 years older than me. I didn't actually find out until years later that he was 25 years older than me. He was a hustler and I wanted to run with him. I thought I was the Bonnie to his Clyde. Statistic show that one in five teen mom gives birth again by the age 20. I fell right into this. I eventually dropped out of high school.

By 18, I was pregnant with my second and it didn't stop there. Again, pregnant at 19 and again pregnant at 21. That's right, by 21 I had four kids and no education. The relationship that started off with wining and dining, soon became abusive, both physically and mentally. I found myself stuck in a place where I had no access to anyone. I pulled away and disconnected from the people that love me. I didn't talk to anyone. I was isolated from the world. My mom didn't even know I was pregnant with my last until I was 8 months pregnant.

In 2007, I had enough of the abuse. My newborn was three months old. My mom came over to visit and bring the baby some clothes. She had been there for about an hour and in walks my kid's father with groceries. I normally got up and cooked as soon as he came home. This day I did not. I continued to have time to talk with my mother. This agitated him. My mom noticed that he was irritated so she prepared to leave. The children and I followed her out to the driveway to say our goodbyes. It began to drizzle. Sixty seconds later, he comes to the porch screaming and cussing demanding that I bring the children inside. I kissed my mom goodbye and went inside. He began to cuss me out in front of the kids, which wasn't abnormal. He was so furious that his food wasn't being prepared. I began to cook with tears flowing down my face. After five minutes, the yelling still continued. I had been packing up for months just waiting for the opportunity to escape the abuse. I promised God that if He got me out, I would not come back. This was it. I called my mom on the phone and asked if she would please turn around and come get me. She did. By this time, it was pouring cats and dogs outside and at this moment I unloaded the closet that was stacked with garbage bags of clothes. I put them into her car. This was my escape. I never looked back. That was it. After five years, I was free. It wasn't all peaches and cream after we left. I had to sleep in my mom's living room with my boys. We put my mom's two couches together and we slept like that for months. My mom helped me to focus on the future. Since I was already a great cook, she encouraged me to go to culinary school. I didn't want to attend school because I knew that I had to provide for my children with no help from their dad. So, I worked at a local deli. That didn't last long because of daycare, or the lack thereof. My relationship with Christ is one thing that continued to grow. I dove deep into Him. He blessed me with my own apartment within six months of living with my mom and right after that I decided that culinary school wasn't a bad idea. I entered and completed, making me a chef. My children began to blossom and I was surrounded by family that believed in me. Today I'm no longer broken but healed. I took time to allow God to heal me from the brokenness that was the reason that I even ended up in these abusive situations. I met a wonderful Christian man who found value in me. He was so impressed by who I was that he asked me to marry him. During the second year of our marriage I got pregnant with another boy. That's right! Now a mom of five boys! I continue to climb up the culinary latter and with only 10 year of' experience the first woman and first African-American to become executive chef since my company Opened in 1923. I made history! This girl! God used all of this for His glory to let some young mom know that no matter how bad it may seem now; God is able to change your story! He will give you a happy ending. My message to moms, keep fighting and keep believing in yourself. With God all things are possible. My favorite scripture has been, "I can do all things through Christ that strengthens me," Philippians 4: 13. You can do it mama! God is able to take you From Trials to Triumph!!

~Camille Robinson

2

HEY TAR-BABY! YOU'RE BLACK! Peasy Head! Big Eyed! You are Ugly! Wow! As I reminisce on my childhood and knowing all I do now, it's no surprise that I became a teenaged single mom. Don't get me wrong, I have good memories from my childhood, but I also have scares. See, Tar Baby, Black, Ugly are all words used to describe me as a child by many people, friends and family included. They would find their comments funny so I would laugh along despite feeling insignificant and worthless on the inside. Growing up a dark skinned, course hair, big eyed girl with meager means. I'm talking about not having lights, gas, or water. Wearing the same jeans three times a week only lowered my self-esteem. The fact is where I grew up, the light skinned, skinny, nicely dressed people were winning (popular)!

I was approximately 14 years old when I began receiving whistles, and hissing from young men, of course after feeling like an ugly duckling for many years, the attention I received was quite flattering. In-fact, my older first love (lover) made me feel special and beautiful, so much so, that even though our first sexual encounter was extremely painful, I bared it and cherished it because emotionally, I felt loved and beautiful. Fast-forward almost two years, I was just about 16 years old and now feeling myself a bit. I know that I have something that boys want. Honestly, I wasn't interested in the boys my age. I felt like they were immature, silly, and didn't have anything (money) to offer me.

My first boyfriend would make sure I had money in my pocket and buy me things, however, our relationship ended when my heart was broken when I learned he took another woman to the state fair. As I shared earlier, I came from meager means and I learned from watching my older sisters. No Money, No Honey! If the guy doesn't have just as much as you or more, don't give him the time of day. Hence, reasons I was not interested in boys my age. Well, I met a man about 8 or 9 years my senior. He was a popular DJ and was interested in me. One of my friends was dating his friend and convinced me that he was a great guy and really into me. We began hanging ou. I can't really say dated because I don't recall him every taking me out, other than meeting him at clubs and sitting behind the DJ booth with him. He began giving me money, buying me things, and taking me to meet his friends. Months later, I'm pregnant, having a baby at age 17 and found out my DJ boyfriend has a girlfriend and a daughter.

I remember when my family learned the news of my pregnancy, I heard the following types of statements, "Told you she was hot in the tail." "She's not going to be nothing." Overhearing these words seem to knock those childhood insecurities right back into me. However, hearing those words from loved ones also brought about a sense of defiance. Not in the since of unruly, but more in a motivational realm. I was determined to show them, that I was relevant, I will not drop out of school, and I will succeed in spite of my current situation. I enrolled in a teenaged pregnancy program called TAPP, where I met a school guidance counselor, who related to my situation.

She was beautiful, well dressed, graduated from college and she had a young son. She held a fashion show for us, taught us how to care and love ourselves as well as to always strive to better our situation no matter what stumbling blocks come our way.

I had to go on public assistance to include Medicaid and food stamps. As a young person still in love with her baby daddy, I would listen to the lies of him wanting to be with only me. We moved in together, I continued to go to school and graduated when my son was approximately 12 months. Shortly afterwards, I was pregnant again and living in a shelter. I recall one day walking, approximately two miles, from the shelter to the welfare office for an appointment to maintain my public assistance. I had my toddler by my side and a baby in my stomach. I will never forget, as I was in line to get to the receptionist, I started to feel very hot. Next thing I know, I was on the floor with tons of people looking down on me. I had fainted. I was totally embarrassed. A few weeks later, I received an approval for public housing (projects). For a while, my kid's dad and I were together, trying to make it work, that is until one night I woke up to loud music downstairs in my apartment. My second child was a couple of months old. I go downstairs to say shut off the music and I find my kid's dad and others sitting around doing drugs. At that point I had enough. I put him out and only saw him sparingly when the kids were at his family's house. I continued to tell myself, you must do something greater than working at Krystals or Burger King (actual jobs I held), so I enrolled in community college.

At the age of 19, I soon found myself in another unhealthy relationship, with a man, who had a good heart but was abusive and controlling. Infact, I had to quit school because of his jealousy and being overbearing. What did I do? I married him, because he was jealous of course that meant, in my mind, he loves me. The day we got married at the court house, the car caught fire while we were driving. I should have listened to that sign that this marriage was not meant to be. We were too young and really got married because it sounded good and others were doing it. After seeing my oldest child being affected negatively by the constant fighting and numerous police visits for domestic violence, the marriage ended after about 1 ½ years.

I recall while working my shift at Burger King one day, I saw a lady older than me at the time with quite a few children. One of them had homework and asked their mom what should they put down as her parent's job. The mom told the child, "Nothing. You know I don't work." The look on that child's face will never leave me. It was a look of defeat. I related to that feeling. I've been there before, the ugly, peasy head; tar-baby knows that pain! At that moment, I said to myself, "I'm going to do something to make sure my boys are proud of me. I don't want them to say, my mom works at Burger King." That's not to say, something is wrong with working at any fast food restaurant. It's an honest living, but that's not what I wanted for my life.

I enrolled in a program to get my Certified Nursing Certificate and got a better paying job as a CNA. After doing that for awhile, I went back to school at a community college, joined scholarly business clubs, learned all I could and obtained my associates degree, which landed me a better job. After a year or so, a better relationship, and twins later, I enrolled in a 4-year college and earned a Bachelor's degree in Business Administration.

Subsequently, I began my career, my true journey with God, got married and graduated. Then I decided to further my education and earned a Master's of Arts degree in Human Resources Management with a minor Leadership. I've continued to further my career, grow in my faith, and enjoy my family. My oldest son is now 30 years old and my babies are 20 years of age. I made it a point to always tell my children, I love them, talk to my daughter and tell her how beautiful she is. They may not make all the right choices in life, no one does, but I want them to always feel loved and significant in life. It took me quite a while to realize that I was a jewel. In-fact, I look back and I am now thankful for the negativity, pain, and un-pleasantries. It shaped me into the woman God intended me to be. A woman who is full of love, gives freely of herself, treat others well despite how she's treated, shares her testimony in an effort to help someone else in their journey, and lives in what I call a "no judgment zone". I am thankful for God's Grace and Mercy.

~Donna Williams

You must triumph over the negative thoughts in your mind before you triumph over the trials in your life.

3

9/11 IS A DAY WE WILL NEVER FORGET. Most people remember witnessing this horrific tragedy on American soil. I clearly remember laying in my bed while watching the live coverage of the first airplane infiltrate one of the Towers. I couldn't help but to think about little Cierra who was to be born on this day, September 11, 2001. Before I continue, let me go down memory lane.

I was sixteen years old and fresh out the pen, a juvenile residential home. I was a very rebellious child, notorious for skipping school, smoking weed and all sorts of debauchery. My mother reached out to the department of social services for help. They saw fit to put me in a facility to straighten me out. It was a rehab for teenagers. I remember lying to all my friend's and telling them I was moving to Texas with my dad for a while. I received my GED while I was there and got accepted in Westfield State College acceleration summer program. This was a way to redemption, so I thought. The pressure was too much so I dropped out with just two weeks left in the program. The professors called my mom hoping to encourage me to return but that wasn't enough. I was a lost little girl trying to figure her way out, but with the lack of a solid support system, I would slowly pick up the same old habits that I fought so hard to break.

I remember this particular summer day as I took a ride on my bike to meet up with my cousin. I see a tan Escort pulling up into a driveway in front of me forcing me to stop. The driver was my soon to be baby father. I don't remember the conversation, but I do remember riding away with a smile and very impressed by his persistence. We had mutual friends so he would shoot his shot whenever he saw an opportunity. This time he would get those two points off the board because I was on the rebound. I had a boyfriend at the time, who was fighting his own demons so that left me feeling rejected. Perfect timing, huh?

He knew I liked to smoke weed so we would chill and talk for hours. We became familiar with each other and the chemistry was immeasurable. He was very supportive and encouraged me to follow my dreams. He even took me to a job interview I had with McDonalds. I got hired so I felt like I owed him more than a thank you. We were inseparable. I didn't care that he had a 5-month-old and another baby on the way with his girlfriend. He was giving me what I needed; validation and attention. I would soon see his true colors. He got into an argument with his girl and took his anger out on me and I promised God that I would never talk to him again. Two weeks later, to my surprise, I discovered that I was pregnant. After giving birth to my nine-pound bundle of joy, I was determined to make a better life for us.

Fast forward to four weeks prior to that monumental day, September 11, 2001. I was 36 weeks pregnant with my second child. I came to the realization that I couldn't account for the last time I felt Cierra move in my belly. I called my doctor and express my concerns. This is just another false alarm, I said to myself, as I have had several false alarms throughout the pregnancy. I arrive to the hospital and the examining nurse immediately notices something's wrong. The doctor comes in for further observation and to my devastation, there is no fetal heartbeat nor movement. The doctor looks up at me and says, "I'm sorry". I looked at the doctor in disbelief. My eyes filled with tears and I screamed and cried out so loud that every expecting mom knew that I was living their worst nightmare. The doctor held me and we cried together. I was filled with so much sorrow, pain and perplexity because earlier on in the pregnancy, I prayed for God to take my baby girl. I didn't want to bring another child into this toxic relationship because I knew it would be harder to get out.

By the time I reached 36 weeks, I accepted the fact that I was going to be a mom for the second time. Why God, would you take her now? I bought clothes, I chose her name and I finally started to love her. And if she could survive my drug use and the physical abuse, then certainly she was meant to be here. While reality is catching up, I have countless medical staff entering into the room informing me that I have to deliver this baby vaginally, with the overwhelming realism that she is not coming home with us. At this point, I am numb, dead to the world.

The labor and delivery room is silent, filled with a powerful presence of grief and sorrow. Cierra Monique was silently born the morning of August 18, 2001. I remember a nurse bringing her to me peacefully swaddled in a beautifully knitted blanket. I still hold it and smell it from time to time hoping her fragrance is still evident. The following day my son who is full of life, comes into the room picks up my shoes and says, "Come on mommy, time to go." After I was discharged from the hospital, I didn't have the strength to go back to my sister's house, where I had been housesitting. I was being abused very subtly before, but when we moved into my sister's house the temperature elevated several degrees. It was a living hell and I didn't have the strength to go back there. So, the next option was my mother's house.

My mother and her church made all the funeral arrangements. It was a beautiful service. I vaguely remember who showed up because I was so numb. As I watched her dad pick up the shovel and cover her casket with dirt, I wondered whether it was regret, relief, grief or contentment that consumed him. Several weeks go by and every day that I wake up I would pray it would end just as quick as it began. Depression was evident. I cried out to God every night that He would take away the pain and help me to find purpose again because I still had my son to take care of. The relationship was over and I eventually became homeless. There was a woman at the church who worked at a family shelter and helped me to get a room. My pride was too big for that, but it was either a shelter or the streets. I had hit rock bottom, but I knew God was waiting for me right there. I was done trying to figure out life and do things in my own strength. God showed His strength in my weakness and I owe everything to Him. I started to reflect the countless times, He spared my life and provided for me. It was time to humble myself and admit the fact that I needed help and I couldn't do it alone.

The woman from the church bought me a bible and I began to go back to church faithfully. I found myself on my knees every night seeking the face of God. Right where He wanted me to be. I enrolled back in school free of charge. Daycare and transportation were free. After about a month and a half, I signed a lease to my first apartment. How things turned around so fast, I owe all to God. It felt good to have a sense of direction and an idea of where life was taking me. Fast forward sixteen years later, my oldest son is currently a Freshman at Howard University, majoring in Business Management and Finance. I am a Licensed Practical Nurse planning to pursue a Bachelor's in Nursing and then moving to medicine. I have a total of six children now and they are all such a blessing. Their nickname is the 'The Team'. You could imagine there is never a dull moment in our home.

If I could convey a message to you, I would say never give up. Allow God to be the captain of your life. Trust me, I know what it's like to be on both sides and God's side is the winning side. Just trust Him with every decision you make. The bible tells us in Romans 8: 38, nothing can separate us from the love of God. Your current situation does not define your destiny. Be okay with asking for help because you are not in this alone. There is an expected hope and future for your life.

~Sheila Barnes

Giving up is NEVER an option!

4

I AM A HUSTLER! PROUFOUNDLY SAID AT eight years old is as long as my mind would allow me to remember. Men and women, ranging from varies ages, has consistently and inappropriately sexually abused me. So called family members, friends of the family, people I should have been able to trust and then everyone else. In other words, people that I didn't know from a can of paint. I was desperately seeking love and affection from anyone willing to give it to me. Yes, that sounds about right. I knew nothing about these men. I wouldn't ask too much information because the less I knew about them the better I felt. Don't ask me why. What a pathetic moral I assumed I had. In all reality I just needed to know the basic. Their first name, how old they were and if they had a job. If they didn't work, they had to know how to get money. I think you get my point.

In other words, a hustler! Why? Because they understood there was money that needed to be made despite the sexual or physical attraction towards one another. They were committed to the game and so was I. This ultimately led to my attraction to guys who were in the street. They had 'the style'. I loved the way they dressed. Pants would hang low showing their underwear with a hoodie with some matching J's! Yessss that was it! I can't forget about the cologne. I could smell it from a mile away. I loved when I embraced him because the scent lingered on my clothing and honey, they were fine. Nice, clean cut, edged up with braids or some spinning waves. Made my mouth water and eyes rolled behind my head.

That was good and all but the lifestyle was accompanied by pain and inconvenience. Two things in particular. The first being street trouble. I found myself always watching out for the police and other gang members. I was afraid that they would think I belonged to a gang because of the men I hung around and the colors I wore. Then there was women and baby momma trouble. I was confronted many times with arguments and fights. That seemed to be the trend. What in the world was I thinking? Putting up with this nonsense! Just thinking about it brings me to tears. I wasn't taught how to properly love and respect myself as a young lady and in retuned I allowed other people to disrespect me and I participated in degrading things.

After years of being manipulated, seduced, molested and raped by men and women, I learned a few things. I also picked up toxic and destructive behaviors. I became extremely promiscuous. Again and again, I asked myself was it certainly love I was seeking? Perhaps it was, because I was a child trying to escape the mindset that was stuck in "this is normal" while being trapped around people who I believe didn't care about me. Although most answers are undermined and recently spoken of, the truth continues to remains. Countless voids that led to me getting pregnant at 15 years old. With all that being said, I will never understand why it shocked people when they found out I was having baby.

I began to experience life at its worse and because I was embarrassed and ashamed of being molested and raped, I had to tolerate what was taking place on my own. But how could a child take on this responsibility? I wasn't quite sure but I knew it was something I had to learn to do in order to stay alive. Back in those days anything a young girl did was categorized as being grown or fast. What they didn't realize was, I was crying out for help. The days became shorter and the nights became longer. Deep down on the inside I was hoping someone would save me form this emptiness. Unfortunately, it didn't happen so I tried to make it happen on my own. That didn't work out to good for myself. Major tragedy I faced day to day.

The comfort I obtained increased and intensified because although I was surrounded by people, I was still abandoned by those I needed most. Endless reasons why I enjoyed hearing "your sexy" or "I love you" because I desired that it came from my father and it didn't. I needed to feel secure, held, protected, and I needed a safe place. I always hoped for someone to love me the way I loved them, possibly even more. Of course, that has never happened. Perhaps one day it will. Can I be honest? It felt so amazing when I heard, "I love you." Even though I knew deep down inside it wasn't the truth, but the butterflies I felt in my heart every time he would say it was like a breath of fresh air. He would look me in my eyes only to manipulate me and yet I believed him. Those few moments seem amazing.

I remember like it was yesterday. I was a freshman in high school. I decided to skip school with some fiends and my boyfriend at the time. Good ole' Valentines Day! As we arrived to our location, my boyfriend and I immediately went into a bedroom. I knew exactly what that meant. He wanted to have sex with me. Many thoughts going in my mind. My heartbeat is racing quickly because the pressure I felt. I really didn't want to have sex with him. I often wonder would this ever end. I was hoping he could read my mind or least my facial expressions and notice that I wasn't happy or interested but he didn't. To make matters worse, I never spoke up for myself. I just went with the flow.

What I didn't know was this was a day that drastically changed my life forever. Trying to prove my love and loyalty to this dude, I had unprotected sex with him and three minutes later I knew things was about to shift for me. I asked him, "What did you just do?" Nevertheless, just like a selfish, inconsiderate guy, he just continued pumping. Therefore, I interrupted his show! I said his show because he seemed to be the only who enjoyed it. I was tired of pretending. I was too focused on how I was going to tell my mother. The very thought of her knowing made me cringe. So many emotions running through my head. I was scared, nervous and heartbroken all at the same time. I didn't know who to talk to or trust. I decided to hide my pregnancy for five months. I carried small and wasn't noticeable. During this time, my boyfriend wasn't supportive at all. He actually told me to get an abortion because we needed to live our lives. I couldn't see myself doing that. I continued going to the doctor check up's alone. My morning sickness became worse and my emotions got the best of me. I remember my mom taking some rice off my plate and I cried! I knew it was time to tell my mother. Distraught and nervous, I begin to role-play different scenarios on how to tell my mom. However, nothing made it easier. In fact, it wasn't so good because the more I thought about it the more I could hear voice yelling at me, and imagining her facial expressions. Okay, I finally built up the courage to tell her. I mean what's the worse that can happen right? I asked my mom if I could go to my aunt's house who just so happens to live 45 minutes away. When I arrived there, I told my aunt the truth. I needed to get away because I was preparing to tell my mom her daughter is 15 and pregnant.

Surprisingly, my aunt wasn't upset. No name calling, which was a normal thing in our family. She told me that my mom may be upset but not to worry and everything would be all right. Next thing you know she was on the phone telling my mother. I wasn't expecting that to happen so suddenly! My mom didn't have too much to say on the phone but when I returned home, did have a special treat waiting for me. I was every degrading name in the book. She treated me with great disgust, and talked about me to all her friends and family members. It was like I was the latest gossip on the news. The phone calls coming and going appeared to be about me being pregnant.

I remember her coming into my bedroom and telling me she was taking me to get an abortion. I told her I did not want to do that. She told me, "Geogette, I'm not taking taking care of no baby and if you think you're grown, you can get out." The rage in her faced said it enough. Since that day, mistakes and all, I have been determined to become successful. In order to provide for my son, I found my fist job at Burger King. I was proud of myself because I made a decision to find a job, call for an interview and be persistent with the hiring process. That wasn't normal for teens, heck for some adults. I was 15, pregnant and working. The odds were counted against me because I had a baby in high school but I didn't allow that to stop me. I used it to build me up. Make me stronger as a woman.

I overhead my own relatives say negative thing about me such as I would drop out of high school. Guess what? I didn't. I overcame the trials and defeated every obstacle in my way. It wasn't easy, however, I was determined. I wouldn't be enjoying my teenage years. Some days I would cry because I wanted to go to the high school parties or movies. I wanted to stay out late and be with my friends but I couldn't because I had a baby. I didn't have anyone to keep my baby while I go out for a few hours. I used the free time I had wisely and decided to stay after school and do make up work or work I needed help with.

I will never forget my high school principle. She has a special place in my heart. What most people don't know is she saw behind the tough girl. She believed in me. One day she pulled me aside, in a stern voice and said, "Georgette, you have got to get your act together. Stop fighting and skipping class. Your baby is depending on you. You are going to graduate high school and become someone successful one day." She then told me, "Whatever I can do to help you, let me know. If you stay after school to do work, I'll make sure you get home." I knew then a change had to take place. All my tears, dedication, and hard work paid off! I had I walked a crossed the stage with my baby and got my high school diploma! The joy I felt is beyond what I can explain. Every step I took a tear fell. This time it was tears of joy! They said I would drop out off high school because I had a baby and I proved them wrong. One day my son will look back at pictures and see he was apart of history in the making. He's the reason I never gave up.

Life continued after that great accomplishment. His father and I seem to argue everyday over foolish incidents. He would constantly lie to me and that turned into flirting and cheating on me with other women. It didn't matter that I went to school with some of these females or the fact that I worked with them. Did I mention a few called me "friend"? I use to wonder why am I really putting up with this? I knew I deserved better.

Every time I thought about ending it, I always thought about my son and the image I wanted to keep. I needed us to be a family, so bad so I continued to deal with drama and neglect. Until one day I decided enough was enough, I was tired of working and providing for our child alone while he kept all of his money and then turn around and have to argue with this guy. I put him out and we broke up. He decided he was going to move to another state. He didn't call or send me any money for our child. Next thing you know I became a single mother. I was angry! He was able to go on about his life and not help me with the child we created together. Days tuned into months and months tuned into ten years and no dad around to help teach my son how to stand up and use the bathroom, how to ride his bike and no support with sports. I watched my son cry plenty of times because he waited for a phone call or a visit for his birthday. He didn't want a gift. He wanted the presence of his dad.

Although I was there, I couldn't fill the void he was missing and needed so desperately from his dad. All I could do is love on him. I would try to spoil him with clothes and sneakers because I didn't want him to feel like he was less than since he only had one parent. I put him in sports and supported what he wanted to do as best as I could. To fast forward at 19, I became pregnant again, this time by another guy. Same story, the only difference was this one went to church. So, I just knew it would better, right? Not at all! In fact, it was worse. He promised me he was going to marry me. That never happened. He left me while I was pregnant for another woman and his family supported him.

No baby shower, no doctor's appointments and no financial help. No nothing. I was beyond hurt and let down especially because he had asked me to have his baby. I was talked about the most in the church and across the pulpit. My mother and sister were hurt because of this as well. The sad part about it all, they never apologized and that's when I encountered church hurt for the first time. Due to my age and lack of maturity in my relationship with God, that situation caused me to leave God. I felt like I was stuck again with another child to raise on my own.

I used to say things like, apparently, I didn't learn a lesson because I was now 23 and I found myself back in the same situation with another dude. A "street dude" this time. He disrespected me, lied to me, cheated on me and the story continues to. I begin to seek God in a way I have never done before because I knew I wanted to do something different. The truth is I wasn't healed and delivered from the spirit of rejection and I allowed this to dominate my life. This is why the unhealthy relationships continued and toxic behaviors manifested. I didn't love myself like I thought I did. In order to heal I had to admit the truth and then change could take place. I had to let go of feeling shame, blaming myself and feeling guilty of the choices I've made out of ignorance. I had to forgive myself because I was hurt and pissed with me. I felt like I failed at life.

My life wasn't like anyone else around but it was

unique. I decided I was going to start working on me because I deserved a chance to live and not just exist. I started finding out what my passions were and what I enjoyed doing. One thing I had a passion for was hair and makeup. I decided to enroll in school. I attended and graduated with honors from Paul Mitchell school of Cosmetology and opened Salon Royalty, LLC. I also have a passion for ministry and decided to enroll in school. In June 2019, I will have my Bachelors in Theology. Today I am 30 years old, an entrepreneur, evangelist and motivational speaker. But God isn't finished with me yet! The best is yet to come! I pray that you are inspired and motivated my story! Know all things are possible for those who believe.

-Georgette Cunningham

5

LIKE MANY OF YOU, I WAS A MOM BEFORE I got my drivers license. I was a mom before I'd gone to a high school party, before I graduated high school and before getting my first job. I did not let being a mom before experiencing these normal teenage events hinder me in life. I refused to let becoming a mom at a young age hinder me from going to college and staying on the path of my dreams. Did the path end up having extra detours? Oh yes! Did I ever think of wanting to give up and settle for less? Oh yes! But, I quickly learned at a young age, if you control your thoughts, you control your actions.

Acceptance.

17. I cried. I cried so much. Mostly alone while I took my baths at night. I would listen to Ashanti's CD and bawl my eyes out! I had Foolish on repeat! I acted up with my Bigmama and Aunt (my guardians) until they let me go live with my biological mom. I didn't care I was going from a nice big suburban home in Texas to a one bedroom project apartment in Mississippi. I just believed everything he had told me to get me to move back after my summer visit. The infatuation of being with an older well known around town guy soon became bitter. Now I was a pregnant junior and he was basically gone!

Denial.

It hadn't crossed my mind to get rid of the seed growing inside of me, for one, I had no money and two I was in denial. I did not go to get prenatal care or visit the ob. gyn until I was around four months pregnant. I thank God now that my child was not born prematurely or did not suffer any major birth defects because of my lack of acceptance to being a pregnant teen.

Going to school was becoming hard my junior year.

I went from being an honor student to the pregnant girl who slept in class or wasn't in class at all. This was not ok! Was I going to finish my junior in high school? The last two months of junior year my doctor advised that I needed to be on bed rest. My schoolwork was sent home for me to complete. Schoolwork was never a challenge before but it was challenging now dealing with being pregnant and having to deal with my biological moms drug induced mood swings. This just could not be my life!

Hope.

There was hope! My aunt and Bigmama. Although still disappointed that I was now a teen mom, they drove all the way from Texas to Mississippi to get my newborn baby and me. I returned to my original school my senior year now a teen mom. I was enrolled in the teen parenting class like all the other teen moms and soon to be teen moms. The teacher in the teen parenting class was one of the most encouraging teachers I had ever met. She encouraged all her teen parent students to go on to college or to reach whatever goals they had. Graduation day senior year we were lining up to walk in and I was pulled aside to be interviewed by the local newspaper on being a teen mom and challenges faced with remaining a good student. It was a very surprising and honoring moment. To this day, I still do not know who recommended me to be featured in the newspaper but that person saw more in me than I saw in myself. They knew I was destined for more in life. I just had not realized it yet.

The Path.

College with a child was challenging. I didn't go to my first choice college. My college search was geared toward a campus with dorms or housing for young parents. I ended up going to a college that had just that but once we arrived, the housing looked like an old jail. We immediately looked for alternative housing. I ended up getting a two-bedroom apartment right off campus. Not bad for a college freshman. The struggle was real, I had to walk miles to take my child to daycare because I had no car. Luckily, I met a young mom who would let me use her car sometimes or she would take our children to the daycare. Co-parenting was going okay. Although we weren't together, I would fly out to visit my childs dad so he could see her. We were back and forth with being together and not being together and that would dictate his support. Dealing with being a young mom was already challenging, but throw a toxic relationship in that mix and you have a recipe for failure.

Lifes curves can come at you very unexpectanctly. Becoming a teen parent is a curve in your lifes plans. I knew I did not want to have to depend on food stamps, welfare or money here and there from my child's dad for the rest of my life. I worked my way up from medical assistant to a licensed vocational nurse to a Registered Nurse. There were other miscellaneous jobs in between but I kept my promise to myself and my child that I would be better, do better and have better. Fast forward to almost 17 years later after becoming a teen mom I can say that my experiences and trials at such a young age helped mold me into the mom and wife I am today. I am well on my way to reaching my full potential in life.

I know how it feels to feel alone, to feel like an outcast at your school, to feel like your life is over. It's not. I believe in you! Don't let the stares stop you from going to your childs PTA meetings and class functions. You may be the youngest parent in attendance but hold your head high and support your child. You will encounter some cruel people in this world but you will also encounter some wise and caring ones. Cherish them. Those who encourage you to finish school, those who encourage you to respect your parents or guardian, cherish them. Take the handouts in life and use them to elevate you, not for survival. Set goals and achieve them. Care for your child and don't forget to care for yourself!

I know what you're feeling.

I believe in you.

Be a better you today than you were yesterday.

You're a daughter, student, teen and now a mom.

You WILL be successful.

Your path to success may take a little longer but it will be worth the challenges.

You are resilient!

-Tamara Allen

6

MY SENIOR YEAR IN HIGH SCHOOL has finally come. My classmates and I had anticipated this day and the excitement of being seniors for a very long time.

At the beginning of the most exciting school year ever, we were all hyped about what the upcoming year was going to bring us. The excitement of having the best football season invaded the atmosphere with confidence and assurance. We began to prepare for homecoming early. We were anxious to know whom the football team was going to pick as the queen.

Shortly after announcing the homecoming court, I was chosen to represent as Miss Senior Maid! I was thrilled to know that once again our seniors chose me to represent at our last high school homecoming activities and ceremony.

As I awakened one gloomy morning to get ready for school, I began to feel quite nausea. I kept pressing thinking it would soon pass over. After I got to school sure enough the feeling passed. Well it happened two more days straight so I decided to mention it to my mom. She made a medical appointment. On that day, the pregnancy test was positive. Here I am a senior in high school (17 years old) and 3 months pregnant. Oh, what a feeling! What will my family, teachers, my pastor, and my friends think of me?

My mom was so hurt and disappointed but she managed to handle it without letting me see the real hurt. This was my second pregnancy. Because I was made to have an abortion, she didn't even try to mention having an abortion this time. Yes, I was against the abortion the first time and no, I didn't try it again just to get back at her. Peer pressure was a major factor. Most of my friends were sexually active so I wanted to be, too. My parents didn't talk to me about sex because their parents didn't talk to them about sex. So here, I was that curious young lady trying to do what my friends were doing to feel a part of the group.

Now, I'm trying to figure out without the assistance of my mother and grandmother on how to handle my current situation. I truly believe that because there was no family support things got worse before it got better. The tension and the disappointment set in. My mother didn't quite know how to handle the shame and my grandmother wasn't much help. Of course, I went searching for comfort, answers and someone to love me. The father and I were on good terms and that was good! He didn't deny nor did he turn his back on me.

We broke the news to his mother. She was kind of disappointed but excited at the same time about her first grandchild! His family knew my family so that made it even better. My boyfriend's family really took care of me and our unborn child while he was attending college.

As the days passed and the word spreaded quickly, things started getting better. No one openly ridiculed me so I had a chance to focus on my education, senior year of high school and my pregnancy.

I continued to work on weekends, go to school and church on Sundays! As I fast forward, I gave natural birth to my beautiful baby girl, named by her father! This precious little one made her arrival on February 20, 1990! Jonique was 7lbs and as healthy as can be for a newborn. We didn't have much but we embraced each other.

Jonique was blessed to have her parents, maternal grandparents and paternal grandmother. Being that her paternal grandmother could not work, she kept her while I finished high school and worked a part time job! Jonique contributed a whole lot in making me become a mature mother. Her father was off to college and had no means of income to support her needs, but GOD!

As Jonique grew, her father and I begin to go our separate ways! I remember praying and asking God to send me someone that will love me for me and not what I could give to them. We were afforded housing in the projects. Behold, the next week or so my husband, unknowingly, shows up at my place of work! April of 1991, we begin to communicate on a regular basis until I felt comfortable enough to introduce him to my beautiful baby girl! She grew on him in no time. He grew to love her as much as he loved me.

John saw a young lady (19 yrs old) that was smart, intelligent, with potential, employed at a local truck stop and taking care of her daughter. As a truck driver for a local company, he would stop by my job (Bee Bayou Truck Stop) to see me every time the company would send him to deliver on the east coast. He began to encourage me to go to school. Going to school was not an option in my book! My mother didn't talk to me about college. Her main focus was for me was to raise my baby. John kept talking to me about school until I started to believe I could do it.

October of 1992, I enrolled at Delta Career College to get a Certified Nursing Assistant license. I continued to work, go to school and take care of my baby. Jonique's paternal grandmother tended to her while I worked and went to school. My schedule went a little like this: Mon-Friday from 8 am-2pm, worked from 3pm to 10pm. The little time I had between school and work was devoted to my daughter. After I received my license, I immediately started a job in my field.

John and I continued to date. He began looking for a house not knowing that he had marriage on his mind. We dated for 2 ½ years. One nice pretty summer day in July of 1993, he came by my job and proposed!!! He "found" me working and proposed to me while I was working!!! Proverbs 18:22 says, "He that FINDETH a wife, findeth a good thing, and obtaineth favour of the Lord." Position yourself to be found! Okay okay l got off the script a little bit! When I think about how God orchestrated the whole thing, I begin to leap for joy. Jeremiah 29:11 says, "For I know the thoughts that I think toward you, saith the Lord, thoughts of peace, and not of evil, to give you an expected end." Things could have been, should have been and would have been much different if it wasn't for the Lord on my side!!!

September of 1993, he closed on our new home! John had his apartment and Jonique and I had our apartment. We never lived together until we moved into our new home. Two months later, November 27, 1993, we got married! Our family was now ONE! I didn't know he promised my mother that we would not have a child until we were married! With that being said, by February of

1994, we were expecting his first-born son, John II. Our son was born thirteen days after our first anniversary. Four years later (Sept '98), our son Joshua was born. We decided to stop while we were ahead! Now our family was complete with a daughter and two sons!

March of 1999, I began my postal career. As of today, I am still employed with the postal service. God blessed us to raise our children in a good Christian home. Our daughter went on to college and started to experience life! She was a bit rebellious at times because she felt like her father like our boys should have raised her. She did not finish school but has a strong desire to finish. Still today, she will mention not being raised by her father when childhood memories are the topic of discussion! I've explained numerous times her father was not my lifetime partner. So does the absence of a parent matter to children? Yes, it does! It means everything when both parents are able to raise children together. The oldest son has been very successful thus far. He has completed college with a bachelor and master's degree! He had the opportunity to play in the NFL and with Alliance of American Football League. Our youngest son is training to be a funeral director and he's a traveling disc jockey.

On March 4, 2017, God shared a vision! From that vision, I'm Expecting God Ministries™ was birthed! The ministry has taken off by leaps and bounds! Its purpose is to educate, encourage and inspire healthy families! We've published a journal, hosted a conference for the whole family, held events that bridged the ages on different topics, and held events of inspirations on all levels. Greater Working Women Ministries has been very prayerful, hands on and supportive in every area! As the visionary, I've been afforded speaking opportunities in a variety of settings.

As of today, I am a wife of 25 years, proud mother of three young adults, godmother of many, former youth leader, devoted church worker, psalmist since the age of 5 years old, a 20-year employee of the United States Postal Service, an author and evangelist! To God be the Glory for the things He has done!

~Shelia Diarse

Whether you succeed or fail is all up to you. It does not matter what people say or think about you. They do not have the power to control your life unless you hand it over to them. You can rise from your trials and choose to TRIUMPH over EVERYTHING!

MEET THE AUTHORS

Tamara Allen

T amara is a Registered Nurse who is an advocate for equality and justice. Motivating others comes naturally. My goal is to inspire many, young or old & encourage them to stay on the path to reach their full potential. Life goals include advancing to Nurse Practitioner, becoming a best selling author and open several businesses with a brand dedicated to my late grandmother (Big Mama) and my Aunt for being inspirational throughout my life. Event planning and photography are a few of my many talents that I enjoy as hobbies. I have grown to realize that it is important to show others you are appreciative of them being in your life. I often leave or text random affirmations for my daughter, husband, co-workers and friends to encourage them and let them know they are thought of. You never know how a simple smile or words of encouragement may help someone get through what they are going through.

I am the mother of a wonderful daughter who has been there through all the struggles since I was 17. I am blessed to have her. To my precious second born, may he continue to rest in heaven. Many thanks to my husband for his continued support and love.

"I'm not what you may imagine to be a role model but the calling on my life says otherwise."
-Tamara Allen

Shiela Barnes

Sheila Barnes is a 37 year old woman who is a proud mother of six amazing children. With four girls and two boys, who are talented and intelligent in their own right, you could imagine there is never a dull moment in their home. Sheila first became a mom at the age of 18 so she can tell you a bit about motherhood. Sheila is a licensed practical nurse and is currently exploring opportunities to further her education and ultimately study medicine. She is an active member at Rehoboth church of God in the music and fine arts department, single's ministry and a small group leader. Sheila also has a blog called Simply6ix that supports single mothers and encourages them to live life in purpose. Her desire is to break the cycle of broken homes and break the barriers that prevent single moms from living their optimum life.

Georgette Cunningham

G eorgette is a single mother to three beautiful children, Rashan, Dominic and Nyasia! Life has taught her that despite your current challenges, not mistakes! You can and will overcome. She has been a victim of sexual abuse, molestation and rape starting at the age of eight years old. Afraid and embarrassed to speak about such tragic events she soon begin to search for love in all the wrong places. Opening the door to rejection, abandonment and loneliness. Becoming sexual active and a run away teen eventually caused her to rebell against her mother and those in authority. Always fighting and being suspended from school, at the age of 15 years old she became a teenage mother. What an awakening. She had no idea how she was going to overcome this BUT was determined to make a decision because her destiny was on the line.

After successfully receiving her high school diploma, she later attended Paul Mitchell Cometology School and exceled the expectations! She also received a Cosmetology Licensed. Now known as Evangelist, Georgette Cunningham, is a woman of God who is determined to dismantle every obstacle that hinders the growth of this generation. A woman of great faith that manages to pour back into our community, she is an entrepreneur, author, visionary of Dare 2B Different ™ movement, youth director and owner of Salon Royalty, LLC. She is also an independant business owner of ACN. She has been featured in EntreprenHER Magazine and one of the top 50 Inspirational Women in the country! As of now, she maintains a Bachelor's in Theology. To God be the Glory! Determined to make a difference NOW! Her mission is EVOLVE. ERUPT. EVANGELIZE. ™

Shelia Williams-Diarse

Shelia Williams-Diarse is first, a child of the Almighty King. She has a genuine love and passion for kingdom building, along with a personal spiritual vision. "I'm Expecting God" is something that each child of God should experience and live daily anticipating and expecting God to do.

She is the wife of 25 years to John L Diarse; an active, very involved, hands-on mother of one young adult daughter and two young adult sons; a devoted member of Faith Harvest Baptist Church of Monroe, Louisiana under the leadership of Rev. James E. Jackson, Sr.; and an enthusiastic member of various community groups and organizations. Shelia is the visionary of "I'm Expecting God Ministries" of Monroe, LA established in April of 2017. She is a Louisiana resident with birth roots by way of Rayville, Louisiana.

Mrs. Diarse is very instrumental in her church. Shelia's love for children and her passion to reach children of all ages is truly a gift from God. She is humble and does not mind sharing any platform given her with other constitutes of interest. She serves as a role model for structured young women in today's society, exemplifying a true picture of God's daily grace and daily mercy. For with each new day He gives us new grace and new mercy. "It is of the Lord's mercies that we are not consumed, because his compassions fail not. They are new every morning: great is thy faithfulness." – Lamentations 3:22, 23. "For by grace are ye saved through faith; and that not of yourselves: it is the gift of God:" - Ephesians 2:8.

"I'm Expecting God" – never underestimate God, never doubt God, never give up on God, never under-anticipate God; but always seek God, trust God, believe in God, have faith in God, living in expectancy of His will, His word and His way.

Camille Robinson

C amille Joy is a voice of hope to the broken hearted mommy. Camille has overcome so much at an early age and stands today as accomplished women.

A teen mom, once a high school dropout, a survivor of domestic abuse, and ultimately, a witness to God's restoration and power! She embodies strength and spews out joy! Through the many trials and hard times that she's gone through she still managed to keep her Joy.

Today, Camille is a Certified Corporate Executive Chef, published Author, motivational speaker, and advocate for women. She is the host of international podcast,"Moments of Joy". She is a Wife, and a mom to five strong healthy boys. She believes that with God, the impossible doesn't exist.

Donna Williams

Donna Williams is the Marketing Officer for Anthem's South Carolina alliance health plan known as Healthy Blue, with responsibility for marketing programs, membership growth, brand management, partner development, and customer relations statewide. She has over 15 years of working in strategic business development, leadership, & marketing for several health-related companies, and served in leadership positions within organizational development programs. Notable her four years as Vice President of The Key 100 Business Leaders for Memorial Health University in Savannah, GA, where she implemented major employee retention and customer service initiatives, which assisted in the facility obtaining the JD Power Customer Service Award.

Donna has been blessed to be married to Mr. Shagari William for 20 years and she's an active member of Tremont Temple Missionary Baptist Church. Her greatest strengths are her creativity, drive and leadership. She thrives on challenges, particularly those that enhance opportunities to reach her related goal. She's received many accolades, awards, and recognitions to include, the Tribute to Community Star Award by Savannah Technical College's Foundation for outstanding contributions to community leadership, involvement, and volunteerism, Partner of the Year Award through Youth For A Cleaner Environment (YFACE), Southern Christian Leadership Conference (SCLC) Community Leaders' award, National Black Leadership Cancer Council's Community Advocate award, Katherine Hall Distinguish Leaders' Award through Safe Kids Savannah and many others. Donna is also a frequent and highly rated speaker on industry related topics.

Donna is a member of the National Coalition of 100 Black Women Inc. Columbia Chapter where she serves as public policy co-chairperson, member of Junior League of Columbia, past committee chair of the board of directors for the Susan G. Komen of Coastal Georgia, and serves on multiple Health Advisory Committees. She has also done volunteer work for the Interdenominational Ministerial Alliance, including heading up the annual Ready, Set, Go, Back to School citywide event, which serves over 5000 families in SE Georgia (2009 - present).

Donna holds a bachelor's degree from Savannah State University and M.A in Human Resources Management from Webster University. In her spare time, Donna enjoys traveling, youth outreach, and shopping.

Chantea M. Williams

Chantea M. Williams is the visionary of I Am Still Somebody™, an organization created to Encourage, Empower and Equip Teen Mothers to be Greater Women. She is the ministry leader of Greater Working Women Ministries, CEO/Owner of Relentless Publishing House, LLC and Esana's Delights Bakery & Catering Company. Chantea didn't allow the obstacles of becoming a young mother at 15 stop her dreams.

There's A Jewel In You anthology series was created with a two fold purpose. First, to remind young mothers that Giving Up Is Never An Option and to show them that it's possible to go from a Statistic To A Success. Secondly, to prevent teen girls from becoming young mothers while reading the life stories of women who faced numerous challenges as young mothers. You can read Chantea's story in volume 1.

She enjoys empowering others to walk out their purpose through Kingdom prinicpals. She will be hosting her first women's retreat, Graced For It, on October 26, 2019, in Columbia, SC. You can register for this event at www.greaterwomen.com/gracedforit.

To book Chantea for you next workshop, conference or youth event, please email info@greaterwomen.com.

I Am Still Somebody™